What Animal Has These Parts?

TAIL

AMY CULLIFOR

A Crabtree Roots Book

CRABTREE
Publishing Company
www.crabtreebooks.com

School-to-Home Support for Caregivers and Teachers

This book helps children grow by letting them practice reading. Here are a few guiding questions to help the reader with building his or her comprehension skills. Possible answers appear here in red.

Before Reading:

- What do I think this book is about?
    - *I think this book is about tails.*
    - *I think this book is about animals that have tails.*
- What do I want to learn about this topic?
    - *I want to learn what different kinds of tails look like.*
    - *I want to know which animals have tails.*

During Reading:

- I wonder why...
    - *I wonder why animals need tails.*
    - *I wonder if any animals have tails longer than a lemur's.*
- What have I learned so far?
    - *I have learned that some tails have hair.*
    - *I have learned that whales have big tails.*

After Reading:

- What details did I learn about this topic?
    - *I have learned that tails can be many different sizes and colors.*
    - *I have learned that animals with tails can be found in all kinds of habitats.*
- Read the book again and look for the vocabulary words.
    - *I see the word **lemur** on page 4 and the word **whale** on page 8. The other vocabulary words are found on page 14.*

What **animal** has a long **tail** like this?

A **lemur**!

Which animal has this big tail?

A **whale**!

What animal has this **hairy** tail?

A **cat**!

Word List

Sight Words

a
big
has
like
long
this
what
which

Words to Know

animal

cat

hairy

lemur

tail

whale

26 Words

What **animal** has a long **tail** like this?

A **lemur**!

Which animal has this big tail?

A **whale**!

What animal has this **hairy** tail?

A **cat**!

Crabtree Publishing Company

Written by: Amy Culliford
Designed by: Bobbie Houser
Series Development: James Earley
Proofreader: Janine Deschenes
Educational Consultant: Marie Lemke M.Ed.
Photographs:
Shutterstock: Lauren Bilboe: cover; ecuadorplanet: p. 1; dangdumrong: p. 3, 14; yakub88: p. 5, 14; Tory Kallman: p. 7, 14; Earth theater: p. 8-9, 14; sweeth2o: p. 10, 14; Oleksandr Volchanskyi: p. 13-14

What Animal Has These Parts?

TAIL

Library and Archives Canada Cataloguing in Publication

CIP available at Library and Archives Canada

Library of Congress Cataloging-in-Publication Data

CIP available at Library of Congress

Crabtree Publishing Company

www.crabtreebooks.com 1-800-387-7650

 Printed in the U.S.A./CG20210915/012022

 In Canada: We acknowledge the financial support of the Government of Canada through the Canada Book Fund for our publishing activities.

Published in the United States
Crabtree Publishing
347 Fifth Avenue, Suite 1402-145
New York, NY, 10016

Published in Canada
Crabtree Publishing
616 Welland Ave.
St. Catharines, ON, L2M 5V6